A look at ADOPTION

A look at ADOPTION

photographs by Maria S. Forrai

text by Margaret Sanford Pursell

foreword by Marjorie Margolies

Lerner Publications Company, Minneapolis

The publisher wishes to thank the Childbirth Education Association and the Lutheran Social Service for their cooperation in the preparation of this book. A special thanks is extended to the adoptive parents who helped make the book possible.

In taking the pictures for this book, the photographer used a 2¼" x 2¼" single-lens reflex Bronica. The film used was Kodak Tri-X-Pan, and the pictures were printed on Ilfospeed photographic paper. The text of the book is set in 14 point Baskerville, and the book paper is 80# Black-and-White Gloss enamel.
Margolies photograph by John Neubauer; used by permission of US Magazine.

LIBRARY OF CONGRESS CATALOGING IN PUBLICATION DATA

Forrai, Maria S.
   A look at adoption.

   (Lerner Awareness Series)
   SUMMARY: Text and photographs answer some of the most frequently asked questions about adoption.

   1. Adoption—Juvenile literature. [1. Adoption] I. Pursell, Margaret Sanford. II. Title.

HV875.F66 1978   362.7'33   77-13080
ISBN 0-8225-1310-2

International Standard Book Number: 0-8225-1310-2
Library of Congress Catalog Card Number: 77-13080

4 5 6 7 8 9 10 90 89 88 87 86 85 84 83 82

Marjorie Margolies talks about Adoption...

Let me tell you a little bit about myself. I'm a reporter. That's someone who tells true stories about people and events. Almost nine years ago, I did a series of stories on children who had no parents—these kids were orphans in Southeast Asia. Some of the children were older, some were handicapped.

Even though I wasn't married at the time, I thought it was silly for some child to sit in an orphanage when I could give him or her a good home. So I wrote and called and called and wrote—for two and a half years! Finally I found a group that would let me, a single person, adopt a child. I now have a daughter, and her name is Lee Heh. She came to me from Korea in 1970, when she was six. Three years after Lee Heh arrived, I adopted a little girl from Vietnam. Her name is Holly.

In 1975, I got married to a man with four little girls. Now we are a family of six girls. When someone asks me which ones are adopted, I have to say "I forget." That's because when an adopted child becomes part of the family, he or she is just as important, just as special, as any other member. And that is the message of this book.

I'll leave you with a poem I gave to Lee Heh on the day I adopted her. I give it to you because it's so special to me:

Not flesh of my flesh,
Nor bone of my bone,
But still miraculously
my own.

Never forget,
For a single minute:
You didn't grow under my heart
But in it.

Marjorie Margolies

journalist & author of *They Came to Stay*

Sometimes a husband and wife raise a child who was born to another set of parents. They make the child a part of their family by *adopting* it as their own.

People who plan to adopt want to love and be loved by children. For them, a family without children is not complete. Sometimes couples who are unable to have a child want very much to be parents. They have a home and lots of love to give, but no children to care for.

Other couples who *are* able to have a child may also want to adopt. Instead of having a baby of their own, they want to love and care for a child who has already been brought into the world.

Children are placed with other families for many reasons. Sometimes a child's biological parents—the parents who gave it birth—are unable to raise their child. Perhaps they are unable to provide the things a child needs to be healthy and happy. Or perhaps both biological parents have died.

In some cases, children are placed with adoptive families because parents are simply not ready for the big job of caring for and raising a child. A very young mother may decide to place her child with another family as soon as it is born. Then she can be sure that her baby will have a good home.

It takes a lot of planning to find a new home for a child. Sometimes doctors or lawyers can make these arrangements. Usually, though, it is an *adoption agency* that provides the kind of help that families need. Workers at the agency are specially trained to do this job.

As soon as a child is placed with an agency, steps are taken to provide temporary care. Doctors and nurses at the agency give each child a physical examination to check for any minor illnesses or injuries.

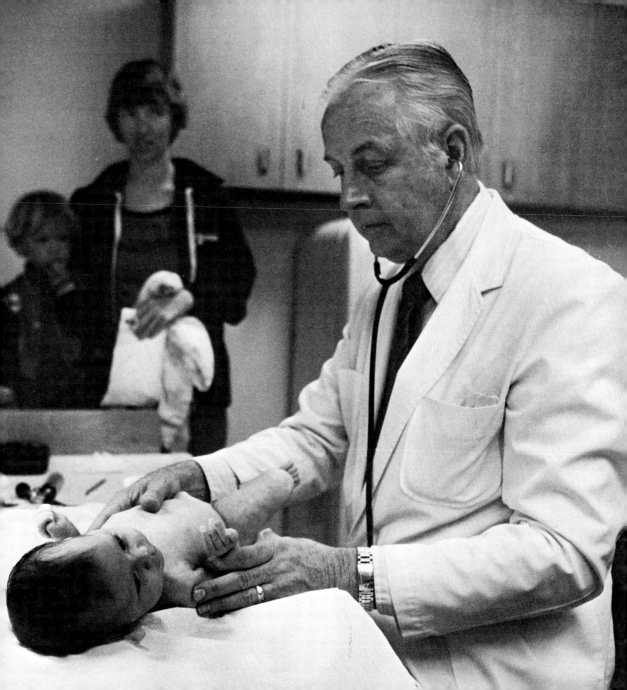

Until a permanent home can be found, a child is often placed in a *foster home.* In this temporary home, the child will be taken care of by foster parents. They will provide everything a child needs until an adoptive family is ready.

Workers at an adoption agency try very hard to place each child with a good adoptive family. Counselors often go to the home of a couple to get to know them better and to talk about adoption. Part of their job is to guide couples in deciding what kind of child to adopt.

Not every family adopts a child whose background is the same as their own. Many couples adopt a child who is of a different race or from another country. Other people choose to love and care for a child who was born blind or who is crippled. Each couple must decide what is best for them.

Not all children who are available for adoption are infants. Many older children are placed with new families each year. Some of these children come from foreign countries and are used to very different ways of life. New parents often have to make an extra effort to understand the special needs of an older child.

In the United States, there are more people who want to adopt than there are children to be adopted. Most couples who want to adopt add their names to a long list at an adoption agency. They may have to wait many years to get a child.

The day when a couple finally receives a child to raise as their own is a joyful occasion. This day will always be remembered by the new parents.

Many months often pass before the adoption is made legal. There is a special paper to sign and a courtroom ceremony to attend. Then the law recognizes what the parents and the child already know — that they are a real family.

The new family will have many years ahead to grow together and to care for each other. They will be just like other families in every way. They will laugh together and have lots of good times. Sometimes they will be sad. There will be many life experiences to share.

They will always have each other to love
and to care for.

Most adoptive parents want their children to know that they are adopted. As soon as children are able to understand, the parents tell them about their background and about the special way they joined the family.

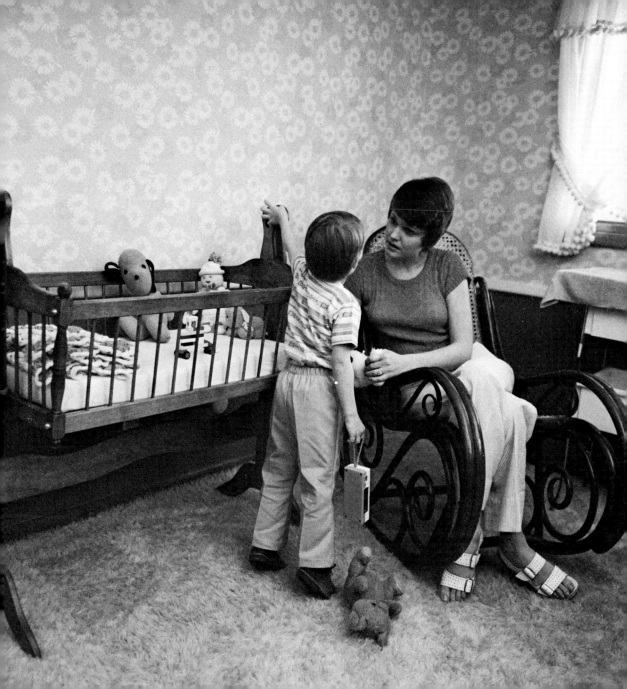

Adopted children understand that their adoptive parents are "real" parents. They are the people who love and care for them, who share their lives with them. And they are the people whom the children love in return.

About the Artist

Maria S. Forrai makes her living by taking photographs. "Photography is a family tradition with me," she explains. "In Hungary, where I was born, my mother became a very good portrait photographer. And here in the United States, my husband and I are establishing ourselves as architectural photographers. Designers and builders hire us to take dramatic pictures of their schools, shopping centers, and office buildings." In addition to the work she does with her husband, Maria likes to photograph people. "I try to show the reality of people's lives in my photographs," says Maria. "I want to capture what they are thinking and feeling."

Many of Maria's photographs have won prizes. They have been on display in Leipzig, Germany, as well as in Budapest, Hungary. More recently, her work has been shown at the University of Illinois and at the University of Minnesota. Maria lives with her husband and two children in St. Paul, Minnesota.